The Art of Restoring Split Cane Fly Rods

A GUIDE TO REPAIRS BOTH LARGE & SMALL

Dougherty

The Art of Restoring Split Cane Fly Rods

Hand Thrown Books
West Newbury, MA
Copyright 2012 - J. C. Dougherty

CONTENTS

The Allure of Bamboo 1
The Oft Maligned & Frequently Misunderstood Bamboo Rod 3
Finding & Buying Vintage Split Cane Rods to Restore 5
How Split Cane Rods are Put Together 12
The Parts & Pieces 14
Choosing the Right Level of Restoration 18
Getting Started 19
Basic Preparation for Refinishing 20

Repairs Large & Small 23
Straightening a Bend in a Rod 23
Cleaning Cork Grips 23
Repairing Chipped Cork 25
Cleaning Ferrules 26
Fixing a Loose Grip 27
Loose Snake and Stripping Guides 27
Repairing Split or De-lamination 29
Repairing a Break at a Ferrule 30
Replacing a Rod Tip 33
Repairing or Replacing Loose Ferrules 34
Re-plating Ferrules or Guides 36
Replacing a Cork Grip 36
Replacing Reel Seats 38
Stripping and Snake Guides 39
Thread Choice 42
Guide Spacing 48
Guide Spacing Chart 50

Final Touches 51
Polishing Bamboo Fly Rods 51
Storing Your Bamboo Fly Rods 51

The Rodmakers brief histories of some of the finest
rodmaking companies 53

v

The Allure of Bamboo

Not everyone should own or fish a split cane bamboo fly rod. Some folks are just too addicted to high tech. After all bamboo only offers a fly rod that warms the heart, bounces the summer sun in a thousand different directions and is uniquely in tune with the rhythms of the rivers, streams and lakes it touches.

Bamboo's unique characteristics made it one of the finest choices for the construction of fly rods. Its' flexibility, recoil and recovery and overall toughness were just the qualities that have traditionally been most appreciated in working fishing gear. Since the very first rod was constructed very few basic changes to split cane rods have been embraced. There's just nothing quite like a well-made split cane rod for performance and "feel".

The fly rod has been around for nearly 400 years but prior to the use of bamboo was most often made of willow, ash or other woods. The split cane bamboo rod we've come to know was perfected in Pennsylvania during the mid-nineteenth century, culminating in the well-known hexagonal design that became so familiar in the early part of the 20th century. It grew up during a time when craftsmanship was the rule of the day not the exception. In a word they are charming in way that big name modern fly rods can never hope to be. Unlike modern, mass produced rods and like fingerprints no two pieces of bamboo are identical... so now two rods can ever be. Each has its own individuality, its own character.

However, the first bamboo rods were made of Calcutta cane which was characterized by thin outer fibers. This cane was prone to infestation by boring insects so Calcutta rods were commonly tempered with fire to kill infestations but often compromising in the process the basic integrity of the rods.

Then along came another generation of rod development incorporating Tonkin cane, native to a small area of southeastern China. This quickly became the standard in the art of bamboo fly rod making where it remains the material of choice. The cane was straighter, smoother and had less obtrusive nodes than its predecessor.

Prior to the 1830's fly rods were generally made of wood and were quite long, frequently exceeding 10 feet in length. Noted rodmaker Leonard developed techniques that created the ability to mass produce rods and a flood of other innovators set the stage for the widespread popularity of fly fishing during the turn of the century.

Part of the appeal of split cane bamboo fly rods has always been their action, which is typically slower than modern graphite rods. They are also slightly heavier but when combined with the lightest of tippets results in a unique "feel" that hooks many an angler for a lifetime. Bamboo is conceded to have some of the finest "feels" of any material. Though light it has "body" and wonderful flexibility.

Diehard anglers who prefer fishing with split cane do so for a variety of reasons, even though the modern fly rod seens to have sold its soul to technology. Some seem to prefer the warm brush with tradition they feel when simply looking at the craftsmanship of an era long gone by. Others remain committed to the point of view that a good split cane rod casts better than contemporary competitors.

Early rod making was a slow business, each rod handcrafted and painstakingly assembled into a finished rod. Most rod builders were at first gunsmiths by trade and one of the most famous was Hiram Leonard who developed the machining of tapered split cane which was then assembled and glued into rod sections.

Inevitably mass produced rods became popular and remained so for many years attributable to their widespread availability and moderate prices. They are however generally not considered to rival the quality of handmade split cane rods. Not all rods, even perfectly restored have substantial value, particularly to collectors who value signed and "name" rods like Leonard, Payne and others.

The Oft Maligned & Frequently Misunderstood Bamboo Fly Rod

With the development of modern alternatives to bamboo in the production of fly rods many misconceptions have taken hold regarding just how sturdy a bamboo rod is or that the split cane rods result in a rod that has too slow an action making it the less competitive choice for today's fly fisherman.

Many anglers still believe that split cane rods are more fragile than graphite rods. Most rods, bamboo or other materials are broken in car doors, or poked into a stump at the side of the trail. Fortunately bamboo is resilient. Split

cane rods can be repaired!
Let's set the record straight.

Many anglers believe that the action on split cane rods is too slow, that the inherent nature of the material doesn't permit it to be as responsive as it's more modern cousins. This may stem from several factors not the least of which is that originally the rods were made from Calcutta cane which was guilty as charged.

Then along came Tonkin cane.

As an alternative, Tonkin, when carefully selected and fashioned into rod blanks can easily match the performance characteristics of a modern rod. Cane is the perfect natural material for rod making with its ability to be planed to exacting dimensions while retaining both its strength and flexibility.

Speaking of strength, another misconception about cane rods is that they are fragile. Here's a test. Take a modern graphite rod, a fiberglass rod (probably resurrected from storage in someone's basement) and a split cane rod. Have a friend hold a door open for you as you walk through carrying each rod one after another their tips trailing behind you. At the appropriate moment have that friend slam the door just catching the tip of each rod. More rods are damaged through carelessness than as a consequence of the fighting prowess of fish, big or small.

Finding & Buying Vintage Split Cane Bamboo Rods to Restore

Nothing short of a steelhead dancing on its tail right in front of you provides quite the angling rush as discovering a split cane bamboo fly rod, dusty and tucked in a far and undiscovered corner at a local garage sale for mere pennies on the dollar.

The first order of business is to find something to work on; the patient.

Not every rod that can be restored should be restored with the expectation that it can return to streamside.

Bamboo, like other materials does fatigue with age and eventually may become too weak to actively fish. Unfortunately it is difficult if not impossible to anticipate in many cases whether a rod that you are contemplating restoring is one which will stand up to the rigors of streamside action. You can however get a feel from the overall condition of each component of the rod.

The greater the wear on the grip or indications of wear in guides can be a reasonable indicator of the rods ultimate ability to be returned to the stream

What to look for? Since you're reading this the assumption is that you're next restoration of a split cane rod is very likely to be your first. So… don't spend more than is necessary to wade into the restoration water.

Not all split cane rods are desirable either to the collector nor or they restorable as serviceable fishing rods. And although for almost one hundred years bamboo was considered to be the best choice for the construction of fly rods it does have a shelf life when years of age combine with neglect to fatigue the underlying structure of a rod.

Although this will be a "practice" rod the greatest likelihood is that even as a novice you'll be able to produce at a minimum a very serviceable rod that will become one of many proud additions to your growing collection of split cane.

Therefore don't overspend. You should be looking for rods that fall into a price range that is something more than the cost of a fast food lunch but don't approach the cost of dinner for two. Typically rods from the era of mass production will meet this criteria. Until fiberglass became the rage in the period following World War 22 these mass production companies were able to turn out rods for as little as under $1.

They were popular in their time, plentiful, widely used and generally available in distressed but restorable condition.

Among the leading producers of these fly rods were manufacturers like Wright McGill, Heddon and Sons, South

Bend, Montague and Horrocks-Ibbotson to name a few.

Many of these rods built from the late nineteenth century came with three sections and were usually supplied with a spare tip. Almost without exception the each of the three sections were manufactured in the same lengths, so rods that you find where one section is a shorter length it is likely to have encountered a slamming car door or overly large stream snag.

That is, when you encounter a two tip rod with one piece shorter than the other it's sure to be a broken then repaired section.

Not that it should matter to you at this point in your evolution as a rod restorer but eventually it may be important to remember that a shorter section can and most likely will dramatically lower the value of the rod.

A short section doesn't necessarily render the rod valueless since any restorer worth their salt will maintain a stock of partial and beyond restoration parts of rods as a source of parts to repair other rods.

These rods were typically of average quality although each also produced a "high" end rod. These rods, like most split cane, were heavier than modern graphite rods slowing down the cast, which in a sport characterized by leisurely activity and action is really part of the allure. Most of the rods you'll be looking at will fall into the 6 to 7 weight range with lengths of 8 ½ to 9 feet. Finding mass produced that are shorter and lighter is less likely, but should you find one it is also likely to be more valuable. In general the shorter the rod, the higher the value.

But while the exhilaration of the find can get your heart pounding there are a couple of things you need to keep in mind when buying a vintage rod.

First and most obvious check the condition of all the pieces and parts.

Chrome plated ferrules or guides for instance that are corroded will most likely need to be replaced. Corrosion on plating cannot simply be sanded out.

Is the cork grip missing chunks or is it dried or pitted? Are the ferrules tight? The sections should fit snugly and the ferrule should make a "popping" sound when the sections are pulled apart.

What about the blank itself. Are there cracks or separations in the any of the sections? Is there discoloring at glue lines? Is each section straight or is there some deflection?

Are all the pieces included and are all the sections of the rod the same length? A two tip rod with tip sections of different length indicates that the shorter tip was broken and repaired.

None of these things necessarily disqualify the rod as a worthy rebuild project but may factor into whether to and how much to limit your investment. Finally what you invest will depend to some degree on whether your intention is to restore the rod for use, display or resale, all worthy pursuits.

Make note of the number of guides on the rod and their spacing. High end, quality rods place about one guide at one foot intervals, as measured from the stripping guide to the tip. If the rod has been designed with two stripping guides then begin the measured interval from the second guide from the reel seat.

Lesser quality fly rods tend to have fewer snake guides than more expensive rods but usually only one less. For instance, a cheap eight-foot fly rod might have only seven guides not counting the main stripping guide.

Generally speaking another two general rules can be defined:

1. Vintage British split cane rods are less valued than rods made in the US

2. Shorter rods generally are more desirable/valuable than longer rods.

The disadvantage of these less expensive fly rods is principally that they do not support long casts as easily as their more expense cousins.

Another way to look at this is that fewer guides create an opportunity for less support of the fly line as it passes through the guides. The weight of the line itself tends to create sags between guides which increase friction and friction diminishes thrust and thrust diminishes.... Well you get the picture!

Although not too many mass produced rods are of higher quality there are a few things to keep in mind when examining your potential purchase.

Pay particular attention to the ferrules which join the sections. If they are chrome plated brass it's an indication of average quality as most mass produced rods employed this standard. Brass is soft and the joint between the male and female ferrule tends to weaken over time. The better choice used in higher quality rod production was a metal called nickel silver which much less common is unquestionably more desirable.

Another way to identify the relative quality of a mass produced rod is to look for nodes along the length of the rod. Bamboo grows displaying sections which are essentially growth rings.

These rings or nodes are the weakest point along the bamboo section. A quality rod is constructed so as to avoid having these modes fall side by side which would further exacerbate the potential for a structural failure. Mass produced rod manufacturer generally did not consider this an important step in quality control.

You'll find rods in a wide array of conditions and prices ranging from completed restored to those requiring compete restoration. Since you're just beginning to embrace the art of restoration it's best to begin with a moderately or cheap rod, probably one of the mass produced rods easily found on eBay or in the bowels of many antique shops.

If you happen to have a rod from a well known maker that may ultimately have significant value once restored it still might be advisable to try your hand at the restoration process on one of the aforementioned mass produced rods just for practice.

A CHECKLIST ON BUYING VINTAGE SPLIT CANE RODS FOR RESTORATION

1. Are you buying a complete rod? If the original was 3 sections get 3 sections.

2. Are the sections equally long? A shorter tip section suggests a broken tippet. This in and of itself should not eliminate a rod from consideration but needs to be weighed against the potential final value of the rod.

3. How well do the section fit together? Assembled the sections should fit snuggly or you may have to replace a ferrule.

4. Are the rod sections bent? Although most bends in bamboo can ultimately be straightened if a section is severely distorted it may be a project beyond the scope of a beginner.

5. Are the cane strips delaminating? Again this should not eliminate a rod as a possible candidate for restoration. As long as the sections don't display cracking or separation within any strip re-gluing is a viable approach.

6. Will it be necessary to remove or replace guides and/or ferrules?

7. Will the wrapping need to be redone?

8. What's the condition of the cork grip and reel seat?

Where to look? I'll cut to the chase. Garage (or depending upon what part of the country you live in "tag") sales and online auction sites will keep you busy if you're shopping for a rod to get you started in the art of rebuilding split cane.

What about the prices you can expect to pay for split cane rods in need of restoration? Ebay advanced searches can provide some valuable data on what you should be paying for a restorable fly rod. Just search completed listings to get an idea of what you can expect to pay based on the price that rods have sold for recently.

How Split Cane Rods are put Together

To make a split cane rod bamboo culms are split and then split again into smaller and smaller strips. These strips are then planed and glued together to form blanks.

The process which includes the wrapping of the guides with very fine silk thread, varnishing and making of the cork grip and wooden reel seat, can easily take up to more than 100 hours for an individual rod.

It is no surprise that some of the contemporary rod builders can charge

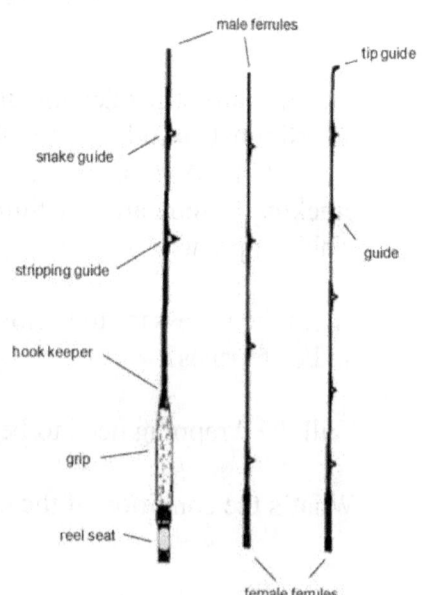

thousands for their work. Collectors of some classic, rare split cane rods have been known to pay more than $15,000 for antique rods in pristine condition.
Split cane rod blanks are first hollow cane cut and shipped to manufacturers in lengths up to about eight feet.

Multiple pieces of cane are then assembled in triangular strips in combinations of four to six pieces of bamboo. Tonkin cane, the bamboo of choice in rod construction is said to be among the strongest of bamboo species. It high density gives rod makers what they are after, both strength and flexibility. In addition Tonkin bamboo is characteristically straight with well spaces nodes. This bamboo species originally grew in limited quantities along the Sui River in the Tonkin region of Guangdong Province in China.

This creates a rod of remarkable flexibility, unique action but with a propensity to distort. As a result most rods are impregnated with various agents to augment their natural strength; rods not impregnated with compounds tend to require higher maintenance than less expensive rods.

The process begins with the cane being carefully split by hand or with a splitting machine then milled to precision taper and other specifications according to the final rod length weight.

Cane has small, naturally occurring irregularities where its leaves emerged. An important part of the preparation of the blank is selecting sections of cane where these imperfections present the smallest chance of compromising the finished rod. They are then removed with special cutting tools and planes.

The cane is cut into strips in specific widths and planed into specific tapers which are then assembled and glued into their rough final form which can either be six or five sided finished rod blanks. Lastly it is assembled with appropriate ferrules, reel seat and grip.

The Parts & Pieces

Beginning with a basic split cane blank rods are then assembled with the following pieces.

Reel Seats

Here's where your reel fits snugly up against and is held firmly against the rod. Reel seats are made of a variety of materials usually comprised of aluminum or stainless steel holders which fit over the flanges of a reel and "seat" against a wooden base.

The basic function is to hold the reel in place and in alignment. Seats are comprised of the "seat" where the reel sits and a mechanism for holding the reel firmly in place.

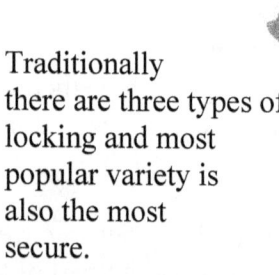
up locking reel seat

down locking reel seat

Traditionally there are three types of seats. The up-locking and most popular variety is also the most secure.

The down-locking reel seat has the disadvantage that the reel sits at the very base of the rod where it can get in the way of the action.

double ban reel seat

There is also the sliding ban reel seat which typically is used only on very light rods and has an annoying way of loosing up during casting since the bans do not lock.

The most reliable reel seats are up-locking, meaning that the top metal retainer is fixed on the seat and the bottom retainer slides up and is locked in place pushed by a large decorative knurled screw. This style of reel to rod mounting positions the reel and its top fixed mounted retainer between your hand and the screw which over multiple casts tends to loosen on down-locking styles.

Cork Grips
Almost all bamboo rods feature cork grips. The cork in grips is graded for quality but in reality does affect the performance characteristics of the rod. A lower "B" grade cork will simply show wear sooner and may display "pitting" where grade "A" cork will typically stand up to prolonged use with less apparent wear.

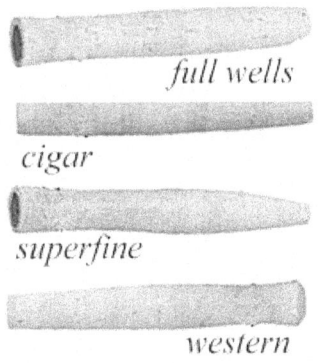

full wells

cigar

superfine

western

The kind of grip you choose to refit in the restoration of a bamboo rod does not have to be dictated by the style that you are replacing. Grips are available in variety of shapes and sizes, each with a purposeful design. Purists are likely to opt in the rebuilding of a bamboo fly rod for replacing with the original style but I would encourage you to consider your fishing style and investigate each style carefully since this is the opportune time to make a change.
Stripping Guides

This guide is the first guide above the grip and has a unique shape and appearances from the balance of the guides on the rod. Typically it is round, double footed and lined with ceramic or in very old rods an agate insert. The purpose of the special insert is to reduce wear on fly lines at the point of most intense stress. Some rod designs will incorporate a second stripping guide.

ceramic stripping guide

Snake Guides

These are the guides that are fitted above the stripping guide and run up to but just below the tip of the rod where another type of guide will be fitted. Snake guides are available in both single and double foot styles. Single foot guides are used in lighter weight rods designed to carry lighter line weights. Conversely, double foot guides are meant for use with heavier weight rods. The better rods use nickel plated guides where chrome plate is typical in less expensive rod building. Any type of coating will reduce wear and tear on guides compared with the austere uncoated wire guides once commonly used.

double footed snake guides

single foot guide

It is commonly thought that using double footed guides make a fly rod action stiffer. Counter-intuitively double footed guides, or for that matter all guides tend to make the section of a rod somewhat softer as they add weight to the rod.

Top Guide
This is the guide fitted at the top of your rod. It is glued then wrapped over its bottom end and onto the tip section. Its design is intended to help release line smoothly during the cast and smoothly during the retrieve.

Ferrules
Ferrules hold sections of your rod together. They are comprised of a male and female section both glued to the rod bland they wrapped with the same silk thread used to attach the stripping and snake guides.

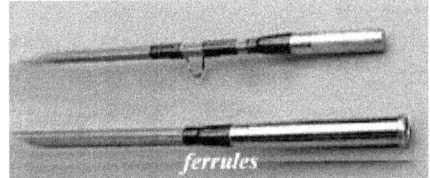

Rod Windings
These are the thread windings over the feet of the stripping guides(s), the snake guides and over the ends of the ferrules.

The windings should be close together with no loose ends showing. There should be several coatings of epoxy finish over the windings to protect them from wear and unraveling.

Winding Check
The winding check protects the cork from chipping where it meets the rod and also provides a finish to the look of the rod.

Hook Keepers
Hook keepers anchor your hook when your rod is not in use. Rod without hook keepers frequently suffer from the hooks being anchored into the cork often causing significant

damage to the cork and necessitating grip replacement.

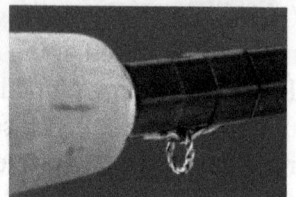

Choosing the Right Level of Restoration

It's best if you become a minimalist in your approach to restoration. Don't do work that's unnecessary.

Generally it's best if you maintain to the degree you can the originality of the rod you're working with. This means replicating original colors; it's sometimes too easy to slip into over-restoring a rod simply because you can.

The work you choose to do, or more to the point the work the rod actually requires falls into three basic categories. Refinishing: This generally includes everything from basic stripping of a old varnish to straightening of the sections of the rod which may have bowed.

In addition refinishing will include rewrapping guides, ferrules and hook holders prior to applying multiple coats of varnish to each section.

Restoration: This is more involved than a simple refinish. Beyond stripping of all finish and removal of guides and ferrules, along with straightening any sections that are damaged or defective the guides may be refinished or replaced as necessary.

New silk wrappings are applied and the existing reel seat and grip are restored.

Repairs: This may involve duplicating missing or damaged parts, repairing loose fitting ferrules, replacing reel seats and/or grips and the nightmare of all split can aficionados partial or complete de-lamination of rod sections.

Getting Started
Stuff you're going to need
A work bench with good lighting
Epoxy five minute fast-setting and/or ferrule cement
Pliobond
Waterproof glue (Titebond II)
Thread for guide and ferrule wrapping – nylon or silk
A vice
Razor blades
Thread tensor for wrapping (both ferrules/guides and re-glued blanks)   A fly tying bobbin can be adapted to the job.
Spar varnish
Sandpaper - a variety from 300 to 800 grit
A heat source: a hair dryer or possibly an alcohol burner
A hammer
A selection of small files
A simple wrapping tool

Patience…

And then a little more patience

Basic Preparation for Refinishing
First things first

Begin by taking careful inventory of the rod's condition.

Make a list of the work to be done and which parts you will need to replace and which parts you will need to recondition.

Check both the cork grip and the reel seat for wear or damage. Sight down the assembled rod and each individual section to determine if any bends will need to be straightened.

The ferrules should be checked to determine if any are loosely seated to their cane section.

Likewise they need to be checked for the integrity of their fit male to female part. If you swing connected section back and forth in a motion similar to that of casting any clicking sounds you might hear are a strong indicator of loosely fitting ferrules which should either be re-glued or replaced.

Although a daunting task, a complete refitting job on an old rod can be time well spent.

Measure and make note of the exact position of guides along each blank. It's best if you take a reference picture of each piece. You should also make note of the width, position and color(s) of the windings and especially the exact distance between the guides. Most basic refinishing requires that all the guides, both snake and stripping be removed.

Generally it is a good idea to plan to remove all guides, both snake and stripping closely inspecting them for wear. If there's any question as to the level of wear it's a good idea to replace them since worn guides can be extremely hard on fly lines.

Even though it is not essential that guides be removed unless they are broken or loose more often than not the finished restoration will be noticeably more satisfying.

It's important that the area you work in be dust free and that you have a clean surface to work on. The guides can usually be removed easily using a razor blade.

If you use a vice to steady you work, which I recommend be sure to tape that portion of the rod that will rest inside the vice in order to avoid unnecessary marring of the blank should you choose to use a vise.

The old varnish can be removed in several different ways. It can be scraped off with using the edge of a razor blade. Many restorers avoid the use of chemical removers for fear that they can dissolve and compromise the glue that holds the rod together.

On the other side of the aisle are those who insist that finishes should not be scraped off since this carries with it the possibility of removing some of the fibers in the bamboo that give it its essential strength.

If you decide to go the chemical route it's best to use

denatured alcohol and steel wool.

There are some citrus based stripping products that are more commonly used on fiberglass rods that can be used to strip the varnish off of the cane that not only remove the finish nicely but do not damage the glue that binds the bamboo strip together that form the blank.

These products generally need to be applied several times in order to succeed in completely removing the finish.

Once the varnish has been completely removed it should be sanded with by a progression of 200, then 400 and 600 grit paper. Begin the sanding at the larger end of the blank working toward the tip

Repairs Large & Small
Straightening a Bend in a Rod
It's not unusual for split cane rods to have bends. Most can be removed with a little care. Often this can be avoided simply by taking the time to dry the rod thoroughly before

putting it up. Also storage in a cloth bag will tend to less any effect from moisture which is the principal culprit in causing rods to take on a bend.

The method of choice is to apply a little heat, gently to the bent area while applying pressure in an arc to reverse the bend. The heat can be applied over a stove burner but you should not apply heat by directly putting the blank over or near a flame. Alternatively, you can use a hair dryer which should be propped up in a way that allows you to have it run without holding it while at the same time allowing you to be able to pass the rod section through, gently heating it as you do go.

If a section has more than one bend straighten them one at a time starting with the most severe.

An electric or gas stove or hair dryer will provide more than enough heat. The trick is to avoid applying too much heat by gently rotating the bent area. It may take several attempts but it's important to work slowly remembering that the distortion in most rods occurred slowly over time and should be removed in a similar manner.

Cleaning Cork Grips

There are as many opinions on how to clean cork as there are fly patterns in the average fly box. You choices run from dish soap to toothpaste to bleach to ordinary household cleaners. Oh, and did I mention fine grit sandpaper?

Almost all of them work, but to varying degrees.

The key is to avoid harsh methods that run the risk of destroying some of the grip material. It's fairly easy to inadvertently remove pieces of the cork during the cleaning process. Fortunately should you unintentionally remove cork there's a way to fix this as well.

Remember cork is a natural material, so potent chemicals or harsh scrubbing can break down the cork and create problems instead of solving them.

The best, most conservative approach is to start with plain old water. If that doesn't produce the result you're looking for try adding a little mild detergent. Run the cork under warm water at the faucet and rub the surface with your thumbs. Then gingerly bring out fine steel wool, (aka an SOS soap pad).

If you elect to, or feel the need to go the steel wool route do so cautiously, stopping frequently between strokes to inspect your progress and insure that the cork is not being compromised. The technique is simple when using an SOS pad, just wet the pad and while holding it in the palm of your hand turn the rod at the same time that you're applying a little pressure. You should avoid scrubbing the grip lengthwise.

The rod blank adjacent to the grip should be protected during any cleaning process which you can do with a few wraps of masking tape.

When you've finished just let the grip air dry, with a little luck it should look as good as new.

Repairing Chipped Cork

This problem was much more prevalent in older rods than with later builds. The addition as a standard of hook keepers made a substantial difference. I remember the cork grip on my first bamboo fly rod looking like Swiss cheese after of summer of tucking the hook directly into the grip.

If you're faced with this sort project there are a couple of approaches that work.

The first method of filing the chips and holes is to prepare a mix of a water based carpenter's glue (like Elmers) and cork dust. Since cork dust doesn't come in bulk containers, or for that matter small convenient containers at most supply shops you can make your own. The reason you use a product like Elmer's is that unlike epoxy the dry time is substantially in your favor.

An old grip from a previous rebuild or replacement (never throw out even a cut up, "useless", replaced cork grip) is a great source for creating the cork dust you'll need. Use a medium grade paper or you'll create dust so fine it won't mix properly with the epoxy.

Start with a small (you'll have to gauge what "small" means based on the size of the repair you're undertaking) amount of Elmers. Add the cork dust a little at a time until you have something that is the consistency of dough.

Apply the mix to the chips and holes with something spatula-like. I use a butter knife. As you work the mix into the holes avoid excess, you'll just have to sand it off later (Don't sand for at least twenty-four hours). Once sanded and your repair complete I recommend applying a cork sealer which you can locate from a variety restoration supply houses.

Cleaning Ferrules
Cleaning ferrules should be part of your regular fly rod maintenance.

Cleaning will help to prevent sticking and make it easier to put the sections together and pull them apart. Another trick at streamside that I've found very effective is to twirl the male ferrule on the skin next to your cheek and nose which for most of use tends to be a little oily. I never have trouble getting the rod sections apart at the end of the day when I remember to do this.

One of the best products for cleaning ferrules is rubbing alcohol. Avoid getting the alcohol on the varnish of the rod. Another product is Vaseline petroleum jelly which tends to loosen dirt or lighter fluid.

To clean the female ferrule you'll need a cotton swab dipped in the alcohol and a little piece of flannel for the male ferrule. Finish by lubricating both ferrules with a little light oil.

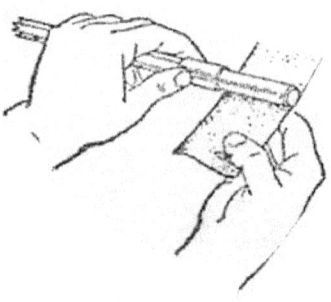

If the ferrule is corroded you can attempt to clean (and smooth) the surface with very fine sandpaper or emery cloth. The trouble here is that ferrules work best when their fit is tight. Sanding the corrosion too aggressively may loosen the fit and necessitate replacement of the ferrules.

Fixing a Loose Grip

Repair of a loose grip can be one of the trickiest things to deal with in bamboo rod restoration. The objective, unless replacement of the grip is part of the planned restoration, is to firmly seat the grip without removal.

Frequently this kind of repair can be simple and is best approached by separating the winding check above the grip and forcing epoxy into the gap.

Sometimes you can cause the epoxy to be drawn into the space by gently heating the grip (hair dryer) just prior to introducing the epoxy. The heat creates a vacuum action that draws the epoxy into the void. Tricky work at best.

Loose Snake and Stripping Guides
Here we're talking about a repair of a guide that is loose not missing. The standard approach is to use quick set epoxy. Generally you can reseat a guide by applying epoxy to thread wraps using a needle.

Once the epoxy is in place you'll need to heat it with an alcohol burner which does not leave residue. As you pass the guide over the heat you will see bubbles rising out of the epoxy. After removing any excess epoxy you should spin the section slowly to assure that the cured repair will be round.

Repairing Splits or De-lamination
Flexing each rod section individually as well as flexing the rod fully assembled should reveal any places where the rod may be split or where sections of the cane are beginning to separate.

Split cane rods can be broken in a variety of different places, none particularly predictable.
Repairing a broken or split section of a rod is one of the most intimidating challenges in rod reconstruction.

With luck you'll be dealing with a separation in a section caused by the failure of the glue that originally bound the sections together rather than a structural failure of the bamboo itself. This occurs under the normal stresses of fishing a rod and these separations are completely repairable.

Normally a portion of the rod section that is separating is still attached. In other words it is rare that a section will separate completely from its companion sections.

To repair splits the approach is to carefully pry the section away to expose the once glued interior and once pried to hold the section apart using something like toothpicks as wedges.

The first step is to remove the ferrule closest to the separation then gently force the split open as wide as it will spread without forcing more separation along the original glued surfaces.

Prop the
split open using something like toothpicks. Once I have the split section gently pried apart I like to lightly sand the interior surface using an 800 grit paper on the belief that a freshly sanded surface will promote better adhesion of the re-glued pieces.

The obvious objective in repairing small cracks and slits in rods is to re-glue the damaged section. Sometimes this is easier said then done.

By far the best tool would be a syringe, but alternatively you can accomplish the same end using a needle as a tool to dip in the glue and force it into the crack. An epoxy rather than wood glue would be my first choice although it's a little trickier to work with, having a demanding timeframe in which it cooperates.

You want to get the epoxy or glue into the split as far as possible before "clamping" the wound tightly shut while drying.

If the crack or split is more pronounced you may want to employ the submersion method. At times the separation occurs at various places along the length of a blank. More often than not separations occur near ferrules.

Next you'll submerge the section in glue in order to soak the surfaces that need to be re-attached. This does not have to be done for a prolonged period of time but long enough for the cane to absorb the particular adhesive you've chosen.

Once the new glue as been applied, the section will need to be bound tightly in place while it dries which to be safe should be at least 48 hours.

Very snugly bind the sections back together using light gauge wire or heavy twine. Wire is preferable since which unlike thread will not adhere to the glue coated surface of the restored blank. If you would rather use thread thoroughly clean the glue from the exposed surfaces of the blank prior to binding the sections together.
These wire or twine "clamps" should be wrapped around the repaired area several times and twisted closed with pliers until snug. Do not over tighten.

First be sure to
wrap the
repaired area
with thin
fabric
overlapped
three or four
times to
provide a
cushion and
prevent
marring the rod surface from the pressure of the wire.

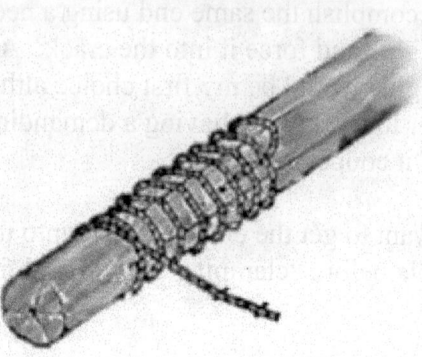

Repair for de-lamination should be allowed to dry overnight before removing the wire or twine.

After drying you'll probably need or want to refinish the section if not the entire rod. Doing so will give you a consistency of finish throughout all the section of the rod.

If you want to provide additional support at the point of the crack you can wind the area with fine white silk thread which when finished with varnish will be virtually (but not 100%) transparent.

Repairing a Break at a Ferrule

What if you have the second to worse break a fly rod can experience?

It's not uncommon for bamboo rods to break flush with the ferrule although more often the break occurs at the tip. Sometimes a section may show signs of splitting. All of these issues can be resolved in the rebuilding process.

In the case of breaks near a ferrule the solutions are similar and straightforward. You'll need to identify a good source of replacement parts in order to obtain a ferrule in a size slightly larger than the one it is replacing.

Reusing original components is an option but generally results in an inadequate repair since the bamboo section will need to be trimmed in order to fit. This produces a "bump" at the spot where the split cane and the ferrule or tip-top have been re-joined.

This method of fix will still produce a serviceable rod but an aesthetically unpleasing result. If you elect to reuse parts you'll need to remove the remainder of the bamboo in the part.

If you want to attempt to reuse the ferrule the old bamboo can be remove from the cavity by drilling a small hole in the remaining material, turning a slightly larger wood screw in to assist in gripping the material for extraction then heating the ferrule while slowly rotating it

This can be a relatively easy job by drilling a small hole into the bamboo then inserting and turning a wood screw to give you a "handle" on the broken bamboo. Apply heat to the ferrule or tip top rotating them as they warm up the glue, then extract the bamboo by pulling the screw with pliers.

Either approach produces a rod which owing to the shortening of the blank will be a little stiffer than it was before the break.

A break next to a ferrule (The worst break is a clean break in the middle of the blank which likely necessitates the construction of a new blank section to replace the broken one as repairs to this sort of break are impractical).

You'll need to start with the obvious; removing the cane that remains stuck in the ferrule. Begin by selecting a drill bit that is slightly smaller than the diameter of the base of the ferrule.

It's likely you will hit metal before you go in too far. This is a soldered piece designed to act as a moisture check and needs to remain. Even though the ferrule is likely to be significantly greater in depth and there is a tendency to want to drill down further on the theory that greater depth will provide greater strength to the repair you should avoid the temptation.

Once you've cleaned out the remaining cane (without damaging the ferrule) you'll need to refit it to the mid-section. The first step is to measure the depth of seating and mark this depth with masking tape on the section you're repairing.

When you trim the break on the section to be repaired the diameter of the section that will be refit into the ferrule seat is most likely to be bigger than the diameter of the ferrule, plan on sanding the section to bring it back to a proper dimension. Be careful not to trim too deeply into the fibers to avoid damaging the rod. It will be easier to sand the section if you place it in a vise. Before you do this wrap the area that will be in the vise with cloth to provide a cushion against the metal of the vise to avoid the possibility of pinching or marring the rod.

Use thin strips of sandpaper (probably 220 grit or so) to evenly sand down the section. It's important to work slowly, rotating the rod in the vise frequently to help avoid removing too much cane from one side or another of the rod.

Sand until the ferrule fits snugly, not too tightly allowing room for glue/epoxy. Ferrule cement available at many sporting goods outlets is probably the best choice in the event that you may need to remove the ferrule at a later date. An epoxy bond will require considerably more heat to break the seal.

If the ferrule you are refitting is not serrated consider replacing the entire set. Serrations act to reinforce and reduce the stress at the ferrule junction. This is particularly worthwhile if you plan heavy use for the rod. A set of ferrules does not have to be expensive and while it will make your repair/restoration project bigger than the initial damage may have suggested would be necessary it will pay long term dividends both in appearance and performance.

Replacing Rod Tips

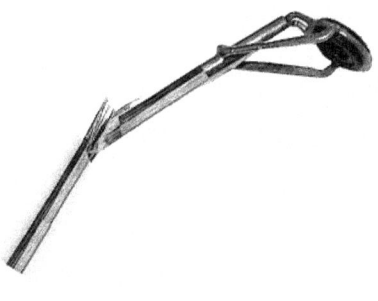

Most commonly the top section will snap off, frequently very close to the tip top guide. The closer the better as this repair is fairly straightforward.

If this is the case replacement with a slightly larger tip top will result in a sturdy repair and a good working rod. The repair will produce a slightly stiffer action in the rod, but should not too adversely effect performance/

Rod tips often get broken off and are fairly easy to replace. If the tip breaks near the end you can get a replacement tip, just be sure you buy a tip with a hole big enough to go over the rod where it broke.

If the tip guide of your rod is loose pull it off if you can. Scrape off any old thread that remains.

First sand the rod tip for about an inch just enough to roughen it up, then use ferrule cement to glue the new tip on.

You can use ferrule cement that typically comes in a stick. It's applied by melting it then dabbing it on the rod tip and then slipping the tip over the glue and end of the rod. Be sure the tip is properly lined up before the glue hardens.

Alternatively, if the tip guide is simply loose you can sue epoxy and an alcohol burner.

Apply the epoxy over the threads that are wrapped over the loose guide. If the threads are unraveled, frayed or discolored you may want to consider stripping the old guides off and starting from scratch with new windings).

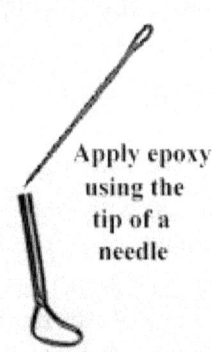

Apply epoxy using the tip of a needle

The epoxy process is the same as described when repairing loose snake or stripping guides.

Replacing or Repairing Loose Ferrules
Given a choice if the ferrules on your rod can just be cleaned or easily removed and re-set with epoxy rather than replaced choose the former.

Problems with ferrules that result in a loose joint are usually a result of the glue that holds the ferrule, either male or female in place drying out and allowing for some movement.

If it turns out not to be dried glue or epoxy but a not so obvious break you'll need to remove the ferrule and either trim or repair the break before refitting the ferrule. Removal of ferrules is like many things in life sometimes easier said than done.
There are two basic approaches to removal.

Pull… or

Heat

Try pulling first.

With many older rods or older restorations the glue is just barely hanging on. If you plan on reusing the ferrules you're removing be mindful that a pair of pliers or vise grips can mar the surface of the ferrules and you should take precautions to protect the surface before you begin. I am frequently successful by applying masking tape before holding the ferrule in a pair of pliers and the rod (protected) in another and gently twisting.

If you're working on the rebuild of an older rod you'll find that some ferrules were attached with pins. These small metal pins run through the ferrule and through the bamboo from side to side. If you discover one you'll have to drive it through with a small punch before you proceed to try to twist it off.

Should pulling fail you'll have to resort to the second

method…heat.
A heat source like a hair dryer is your best bet. Heat guns and open flames from alcohol burners can be too aggressive. Using these can result in permanently discoloring the ferrule or the surrounding bamboo. In any event proceed slowly and alternatively continue to try twisting the ferrule to see if it is loosening. Use an old leather glove or oven mitt to avoid the obvious.

Use pliers to pull the ferrule. Don't use a pair of gloves as the amount of heat necessary to dissolve the glue will make the rod too hot even for the glove-protected hand. Also don't twist. Twisting the hexagonal design of the rod increases the risk of unintentional damage to the blank along the seams.

Some ferrules are serrated which will slow you down but with a little patience you should be able to produce the same result. If this were easy it wouldn't be so much fun!

Re-plating Ferrules and Guides
Not necessarily for the faint of heart but….

If you're interested it's fairly straightforward to re-plate ferrules or guides allowing you to preserve originals.

The equipment for re-plating a set of ferrules and guides can be purchased for about the same cost as a replacement set of ferrules and guides. Re-plating a male ferrule will help to tighten up the fit. The plating solution normally provided with kits should re-plate about fifty or more sets. If your need is for copper or chrome re-plating these solutions can be obtained separately.

I've used these re-plating kits for a number of rods which

have subsequently been subjected to a number of hard outings and they seem to wear extremely well.

Re-plating can be done either by swabbing the pieces with the provided solutions using an applicator or by immersing them in the solution. The immersion technique generally requires that the rod is undergoing a pretty thorough restoration and that the ferrules and guides have been removed. Immersion is more likely to result in a more uniform coat.

The former and simpler way is to dip an applicator into the solution and then apply it to the piece you're restoring. You'll need to rough the surface up to begin with steel wood then clean with denatured alcohol. For very loose ferrule fits you may need to apply more than a single coat, roughing and cleaning between applications.

Immersion kits are generally more expensive. One I've used comes with a small transformer, a clip and a jack, a bottle of nickel plating solution, and a piece of tubing with some fabric to wrap around it for an electrode.

The ferrule is suspended in the plating solution in a glass. Then the set-up is connected to the electrical connectors. The transformer is plugged into the wall and current is provided for two minutes. Temperature of the solution is important and it will need to be warmed to about 110 degrees.

Most of the kits provide a nickel-plating solution, and although nickel is harder than nickel-silver it works well for plating ferrules.

I'm not sure how well the "swab" kits work utilizing the

immersion technique. Immersion kits are designed specifically to respond to the electric power provided by the transformers they supply. They also use more powerful rectifiers.

So swab kits for most restorers work fine and are far easier to use.

Replacing a Cork Grip

The hardest part of replacing a cork grip is getting the old one off without damaging the reel seat or underlying cane. Removal is nothing more than applying razor blade, Dremel or hack saw blade to unwanted grip with particular attention being paid to avoiding damage to the underlying blank.

Once the old grip is removed you're ready to refit with the new. If you have a 2 or 3 piece rod with no guides on the bottom section you life will be easier. Otherwise you need to remove the guides first. In this case the grip can simply be drilled out to size and should slide epoxy at your side into place.

Sometimes it gets a little more complicated and rarely the solution means having to split the new grip into two halves and sandwich-like epoxy them into place.

Replacing Reel Seats

Heat is the tool that is pretty much a given when fixing a reel seat. More often than not the reel seat will contain an element of wood in which case you have to proceed extremely carefully.

If you must use flame use an alcohol burner which should minimize damage. Other flames run the risk of leaving permanent residual burn marks. I still prefer a hair dryer which can muster up pretty intensive BTUs so you still have to be very careful. The idea is to apply just enough heat to create a loose bond. Then apply pressure (generally twisting pressure works best) instead of continuing with heat.

The objective of course is to heat it up until it loosens and can be pulled off. The heat should make the epoxy inside break down and that combined with a gentle or not so gentle tug should separate reel from cane.

If your objective is to replace the reel seat then you can pull all the stops, get out the Dremel/hack saw/razor blade and go to work. Just be careful not to damage the blank in your zeal to get the job done.

When it appears that the old reel seat and or grip are in need of replacement removal of course is the first step. Generally you can achieve this by heating the seat in order to soften the cement.

Once you've pulled the seat off clean the blank where you epoxy the old or new seat. Occasionally you will be faced with a damaged blank but sanding and if necessary filling with wood filler should get you ready for replacing the seat.

The seat (new or old) should be put back on with epoxy. Apply it to the inside of the reel seat and push the seat onto the blank using a twisting motion that will ensure that the epoxy is spread evenly around the blank.
Single piece replacement grips are available but many rebuilders prefer to build up the grip using cork disks, a more traditional approach and certainly more labor intensive. Glue is applied between applications of the rings which are fitted tightly and when dry are sanded into their

final shape.

Stripping and Snake Guides – Wrapping, Winding, Whipping
At last something easy.

Replacing snake guides or a stripping guide is easy. Achieving good looking wraps is a matter of practice.

Before you begin winding you'll have to devise some method of creating continuous tension on the thread during the process. A very rudimentary way to achieve this is to put the spool of thread in an empty glass then pass the thread through the middle pages of a heavy book on its way to the rod blank. This creates tension without having to manage a spool that is spinning out of control across the floor.

simle wrapping tool

Or
A simple wrapping tool can be adapted by using a fly tying bobbin to achieve thread tension along with a simple V-notched wood holder like the one shown. Mine was constructed using ¾ inch pine for the base.

The base can be any length but I would suggest a minimum

of 10 inches with a width of at least 5 inches. The verticals on the one I made and have been using for years measure 4 x 7 inches. Pretty much any dimension you choose will work.
If you do construct a rod blank holder be sure to line the V sections with felt or a suitable substitute to protect the rod section as it turns.

Wraps are just silk thread wound over the foot (single or double) of the guide that anchors the guide to the fly rod sections.

The wrap is then finished with varnish or if you are concerned that varnish may discolor the thread first with a sealer then varnish..

When wrapping with nylon thread I use epoxy for the finish, when building or repairing bamboo rods with silk, varnish is usually used.

One distinct advantage of modern nylon threads over their predecessors is that they are color-fast eliminating the need for additional special products to protect the color finish.

Nylon thread is typically used with graphite and fiberglass blanks, silk is the thread of choice for bamboo rods and their repairs. Thread in size A is best. If you use a finer thread you're more likely to leave gaps in the windings. Conversely heavier threads tend to look too bulky in the finished product.

You'll have to make a choice as to whether you want to wrap the guides and tip top into their assigned position before or after varnishing the rod. I prefer to complete varnishing the rod sections before beginning to wrap in the guides.

Some varnishes will not produce the sort of finish on thread they produce on cane. True-Oil for instance is one of those finishes. Also if you were to wrap first then varnish you'll leave small sections of unvarnished bamboo just below the treads.

Wrapping is where the real art of restoring split cane rods kicks in. Practice, practice, practice!

A colorful presentation and crisp workmanship will show off your finished restoration in its finest light.

Even the smallest mistakes in wrapping seem to jump off the rod. Best part of bamboo restoration? Cut the wrap off and do it again.

Thread Choice
Whatever thread you choose it should have some tensile strength. Most cotton threads are too weak to be serviceable for the purpose of wrapping in ferrules or guides.

Threads can be very expensive and come in an almost endless variety of colors and thicknesses. They are graded from A to D with A being the thinnest available. Generally you will want to restore your rods using a fairly thin thread since thicker threads tend to produce a thick looking finished to the final restoration.

The rod you are restoring may have originally come with several narrow windings between guides. These were added in order to provide additional strength as the rod was flexed in normal use.

One of the most important characteristics in the choice of a winding thread is tensile or ultimate strength. Tensile strength is the maximum stress that a material can withstand before breaking. Generally cotton threads are too weak to withstand the rigors of rod construction and therefore rod use. You can get a good feel for the strength of a thread simply by trying to break it. An appropriate thread should put up a fuss about breaking. Pure nylon or a blend with high nylon content will usually make a suitable winding thread.

It's possible to purchase threads that have alternating colors resulting in some very interesting combinations as you wrap. It should also be noted that most modern thread are color fast eliminating the need for the addition of a color preservative as a final step.

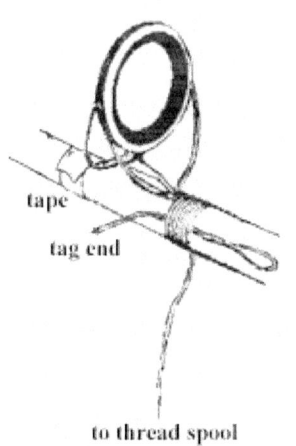

Step one...removing the old guides. It's important that you mark the position of the old guides first. Then using a razor blade carefully slice through the old wrappings. The old thread and epoxy usually fall easily away.

In the event that old guides are missing or you're working with a rod blank that's already stripped of its guides the easiest way to position new guides is to take another rod of the same length, lay it alongside the bland you're restoring and mark for similar placement. No similar rod? Ok. Figure about one guide (including the stripping guide) per foot of rod.

43

The interval between guides actually decreases slightly as you move toward the tip.
You have a choice of how tight to wind the thread. Basically once wrapped the guide should move slightly. If they don't move at all they are wrapped too tight and potentially could compromise the rod blank. Snug is the word.

You'll also need for the wrapping to be loose enough for you to be able to pull the tag end of the thread through to finish off. Let the epoxy do the real work of holding the guide.
The first step is to lay the guide in position then lightly tape one foot so it remains in place. Double check to make sure the guides line up properly.

Masking tape works well to temporarily hold the guides in position. Also mark both the beginning and ending of the length of wrap you intend with a small pencil mark.

Remember more is not always better. The longer the wrap the more likely the rod will be stiffer.

Be careful to avoid any gaps between the thread.

You should never overlap your wrappings. If you have a slight gap as you begin you can adjust by pushing the threads together as you go along. This is an excellent way to get your fingernails involved in the project.

Make a loop in the thread longer than the length of the wind you will complete. Lay the loop alongside the guide foot with the tag end facing toward the eye of the guide and extending at least ½ inch beyond the guide along the rod.

When you finish winding the thread you'll cut the thread to the spool and put the cut end of that thread through the loop. Next pull the original tag end which will draw the newly cut end back up under the winding and finish things off.
Many believe that you should coat the windings with a color preserver to prevent the varnish or epoxy from altering the color of the thread.

Preservers work by preventing varnish or epoxy from being absorbed into the thread, an essential to creating a tightly wrapped guide. Generally varnish or epoxy will darken the color of the thread slightly, which you can simply anticipate in the selection of the thread you will use.

The length of the wrappings is an artistic call but I would go at least ¼ inch beyond the end of the guide foot onto the rod.

Finally apply spar varnish which provides excellent protection from water and sun.

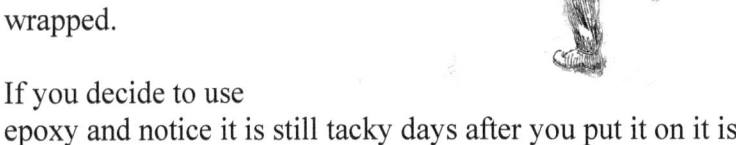

As you apply the varnish make sure to rotate the rod to avoid drips and runs in the wrappings.

Ferrules should also be wrapped.

If you decide to use epoxy and notice it is still tacky days after you put it on it is likely it will never cure properly. Most likely the tackiness is the result of improper mixing of the hardener and resin. I'd like to tell you there's an easy solution. There isn't. Start over. No amount of time will cure this problem.

Refinishing: About Varnishing

In order to prevent the possibility of discoloration whippings should be sealed prior to varnishing.

Sealing products are both generally available and reasonable and it's a step you should not skip.

Applying three coats of the sealant is best and you should wait until the third coat is completely dry before applying the varnish.

Finishing the rod with varnish is also a multi-coat process. Marine varnishes are best and my preference is one that produces a satin finish.

Some restorers thin the varnish before applying it to the rod, some prefer to use a brush, others their finger, still others submerge the rod in a varnish bath.

Whatever technique you choose it will make your life a little simpler if you apply the varnish in sections; between guides rather than to the entire rod, letting the section dry before moving on. This just makes handling the freshly varnished rod easier.

When it comes to varnishing the best choice is the one that works for you.
Check between coats for imperfections which if found can be removed using fine sandpaper if necessary.

The mortal enemy of bamboo as it is with most wood is that over time they dry out. Split cane fly rods are no exception. One way to minimize this process is to make sure the varnish on the cane is always in good condition. When necessary the old varnish should be completely removed and reapplied to insure complete water-tight coverage. Spar varnish can provide a particularly effective barrier to water.

Some anglers keep a little linseed oil handy and apply a thin coat prior to fishing the fill any small imperfections in the finish. You can accomplish the same thing with a little WD40 which is a lot easier to use and gets the job done.

If you choose to sand between coats (many polyurethane varnishes cover very well with just one coat) consider using the wet/dry variety of papers they use in auto body work. These papers are extremely fine but are designed to simply "rough" a tiny fraction of the surface of the varnish in preparation for the next coat.

The key to any varnishing work is patience. Be prepared to let even thinly applied coats dry for days, not hours between applications.

If you experience bubbling in the finish of your rod it may be the result of the tools you're using to apply the varnish. Brushes are notorious for creating irregularities in the surface of varnish work. Given the rather limited surface area you're working with you may want to consider applying the varnish with your fingertip.

Another way to attack the bubble problem is to apply a gentle heat from an alcohol burner which will cause any bubble to expand and move to the surface.

In addition finishing oil applied as a last step can produce a look that you can expect to be proud of. The oil should be carefully rubbed into the surface of the rod beginning at the butt section and working toward the tip. Once applied allow the oil to dry thoroughly before proceeding to apply several more coats.

Between coats very fine rubbing compound will add to the quality of the final finish. The number of coats a rod will need is a judgment call but generally three to five should be enough.

Guide Spacing

The general idea in guide spacing is to space the guides in an effort to distribute the load or stress that angler's encounter both in casting a line as well as in playing a fish once hooked. Placed correctly guides will keep the line in a comfortable contour with the rod as it is flexed.

A secondary goal of guide placement is to minimize friction so using no more guides than is absolutely necessary is important.

Fewer guides = less friction

You may want to consider placing guides in different positions than the original. The placement of guides effects rod performance and since casting and fishing techniques vary from person to person real customization of a rod to an individual depends on understanding the role placement plays.

Where guides are placed on a rod is not arbitrary. The proper placement plays an essential role in helping to distribute the load along the rods length and works to maximize performance. Basically, the guides are acting to transfer the stress on the rod from a cast or the load of having a fish on from the tip to the butt section of the rod. Guide spacing also takes into account the type of fishing the rod is intended to do so a saltwater or steelhead rod will have different guide spacing than a fly rod destined to do battle with their smaller cousins.

There are no hard and fast rules but a couple of things can be kept in mind.

As a rule of thumb a rod will have one more guide that the total length of rod measured in feet. In other words a seven foot rod would typically have eight guides; an eight footer nine guides. The reason this is not hard and fast as a rule is the decision when working for instance with a seven and a half foot rod.

Guides are counted beginning with the first guide below the tiptop. The stripping guide, the one closest to the reel seat will typically be about 28 to 30 inches from the bottom of the reel seat.

FLY ROD GUIDE SPACING CHART

by rod length

Rod Length	1st guide	2nd guide	3rd guide	4th guide	5th guide	6th guide	7th guide	8th guide	9th guide	10th guide	11th guide	12th guide	13th guide
6 ft	3.5"	7.5"	12"	17"	22.5"	28.5"	35"						
6 1/2 ft	3"	6"	9.5"	13.5"	18.25"	24"	30.5"	38"					
7 ft	4.625"	10.75"	17.875"	25.625"	34.125"	43.250"	51.375"						
7 1/2 ft	4"	9.5"	15.750"	23.250"	31.750"	41.125"	51.375"	52.875"					
8 ft	4.5"	9.625"	16"	23.125"	30.625"	38.625"	48"	58.875"					
8 1/2 ft	4"	9.5"	16.250"	23.750"	31.75	40.375"	49.375"	59.5"	70.750"				
9 ft	4"	9"	15"	22"	29.625"	37.625"	46.250"	55.125"	65"	76"			
9 1/2 ft	4"	8.875"	14.5"	21.125"	29.125"	37.5"	47"	56.875"	68"	80"			
10 ft	4.125"	9.125"	14.5"	20.750"	27.5"	34.5"	42.250"	50.250"	56.750"	68.250"	77.5"	88"	
10 1/2 ft	4.625"	10.375"	16.250"	22.625"	29.375"	36.375"	43.750"	51.625"	59.875"	69"	78.250"	88.250"	98.625"

by line weight

Line Weight	Rod Length	Rod Pieces	1st guide	2nd guide	3rd guide	4th guide	5th guide	6th guide	7th guide	8th guide	9th guide	10th guide	11th guide
3-4 wt	7ft	2	4"	8.750"	14.375"	20.750"	28"	35.875"	44.625"	54.125"			
4-5 wt	8ft	2	5"	10.250"	15.5"	21.375"	27.375"	33.750"	40.5"	56.5"	66"		
5-6 wt	8 1/2 ft	2	4.5"	9.875"	16.125"	23.250"	31.250"	40.250"	50"	72"			
7-9 wt	9 ft	2	4.5"	9.750"	15.750"	22.375"	29.750"	38"	46.875"	56.375"	66.750"	77.875"	
10-13 wt	9 ft	2	4.5"	9.750"	15.750"	22.375"	29.750"	38"	46.875"	56.375"	66.750"	77.875"	

guide spacings are a matter of personal preference and can vary both by rod composition as well as the fishing techniques of individual anglers these spacing recommendations are exactly that; recommendations

Final Touches
Polishing Bamboo Fly Rods
Split cane bamboo fly rods, many individually crafted are as much art as utilitarian tools of the angling trade. Keeping them dry is essential. Keeping them clean a must! Bring them to the next plateau... polish them. A good wax job is hard to beat. Furniture polish not only helps keep them dry by sealing any minute imperfections in the finish, it also periodically cleans the surface and brings out the best in the character of the bamboo.

Storing Your Bamboo Fly Rods
Before you put your rod up make sure to dry it. Rod socks are excellent since they keep the sections separate and tend to absorb any atmospheric moisture that happens to penetrate the rod case.

Keep the rod case away from temperature extremes, particularly heating ducts, radiators, attics and basements. Lay the rods down rather than standing up for storage

The Rodmakers

On the off chance that lady luck decides to tag along with you on your quest for that perfect rod restoration project and you stumble upon what might be a real jewel in the rough it might be helpful to be familiar with some of the more prominent rodmakers.

This could help to minimize unnecessary blubbering and stuttering as you attempt to negotiate a final deal.

So here are brief histories of some of the rodmakers along with some hints on identifying the rods, from the most sought after to some more pedestrian that serious restorers find while rummaging through dusty corners and forgotten byways.

The list is not complete nor does it attempt to highlight just the finest rods made, but rather to give some guidance to the uninitiated. These guys made and some still make some pretty good rods.

Dickerson Rods
Dickerson Rods, namesake of company founder Lyle L. Dickerson were introduced post-depression, crafted in a small one man shop in Detroit, Michigan. These bare-boned, straightforward looking rods were slow to gain fame as they were being produced far from the epicenter of split can rod making in the first half of the twentieth century, the Catskills.
The rods proved, however to be every bit the work of a serious craftsman.

His earliest rods are dated around the 1930's, were three piece and typically of moderate taper. Eventually he came to be known and appreciated for a faster action two piece rod.

A friendship with a sporting writer named Bergman who began distributing rods for Dickerson resulted in some of his rods being marked "Dickerson-R.B" or "Dickerson-Bergman".

You may also come across rods marked "Dickerson-Leitz" or "Dickerson-Detroit" which he also used.

The inscribed model numbers describe both the length of the rod as well as the diameter of the ferrule. So model number 8015 would be an eight foot rod with ferrules of size 15. He used down-locking reel seats almost exclusively of nickel silver and walnut. Most rods featured brown wraps with black tipping.

E.W. Edwards & Sons
E. W. Edwards worked for the Leonard Rod Company in Central Valley, New York as a novice rodmaker, training at the right hand of Hiram Leonard. Along with a co-worker of some eventual notoriety, F. E. Thomas he left Leonard only to join and start the Thomas, Edwards & Hawes Rod Co.

Soon Hawes is replaced by Edward Payne and the company becomes Thomas, Edwards & Payne. If you are lucky enough to come across a Kosmic rod made by this short lived company you've found a very scarce rod, as few were made.

Both Edwards and Thomas shortly left only to rejoin in Bangor, Maine with a newly formed rodmaking company, the Thomas & Edwards Rod Co. This new venture mainly produced private label rods. Look for names like Empire

City and Von Lengerke & Detmold.

By 1900 the two had split once again and Edwards started the E. W. Edwards Rod Co. His son Leon, joined him after several years and eventually took over when Edward passed away. The company continued making rods into the 1950's when a combination of the use of fiberglass technology that emerged during the war and difficulty obtaining suitable cane choked rod production and brought the company to an end.

The Edwards name, now long associated with the highest quality workmanship in rodmaking was kept alive as sons, Bill and Leon continued the tradition.

F.E. Thomas Rod Company
Fred Thomas began making rods under his name in the 1890's. He earlier had associated with rodmaking legends Hiram Leonard, Edward Payne and Eustis Edwards.

He began as an apprentice at the H. L. Leonard Rod Co., in Bangor, Maine. In 1983 he left Leonard and along with Edwards and Payne began making rods under the name Thomas, Edwards and Payne.

A short five years later Thomas and Edwards left Payne moving to Thomas' home of Brewer, Maine to continue rodmaking under the name Thomas and Edwards Co. The partnership didn't last long, selling a limited number of rods under names like Empire City Tackle when Thomas went it alone.

This was the beginning of the F. E. Thomas Rod Co.

Garrison Rods

Garrison came to rodmaking after a career in engineering with the New York Central Railroad. After getting laid off necessity and interest drew him to rodmaking and he made his first in the late 1920's and began selling them by 1930. Although he continued to pursue work as an engineer he simultaneously worked to develop a unique, methodical approach to rod making the central premise of which was that when loaded a rod should deliver constant stress.

His rods were named beginning in 1931 using the letter of the alphabet. A rod labeled C-8-12, for instance would be one made in 1933 (the third year he used the system), one eight feet in length, and the twelfth rod produced that year.

He good a little luck when John Alden Knight, a famous writer after using one of Garrisons rods invited him to lecture on rodmaking at the New York Angling Club, producing a rush of sales to its' members.

Leonard Rod Company
Leonard rods are among the finest quality ever produced and have enjoyed that position of excellence since the company's founding by Hiram Leonard.

For many, Hiram Leonard is considered the father and master rod builder of the modern fly rod. Many of the biggest names in fly rod making began their careers under the tutelage of Hiram and the Leonard Rod Company.

It was in 1869 that Hiram designed then built his first fly rod, which at the suggestion of a friend he showed to a sporting goods company in Boston. The produced an immediate order leading eventually to his development of the six strip rod we are so familiar with today.

Hiram was the first rodmaker using compound tapers which he calculated mathematically. He was also the first to discover Tonkin cane. His rods are among the most highly prized and valued by collectors.

The Gillum Fly Rod Company
Harold "Pinky" Gillum got his start in rod building through a connection with Eustis Edwards. He was also a friend of Jim Payne. He was a carpenter by trade but gravitated to rod making and eventually along with his wife Winnie started the Gillum Fly Rod Company. He met Winnie when he worked at Orvis.

After they married they moved to Ridgefield, CT where they started building rods.

The consensus is that his rods copied those of Garrison and Payne to a substantial degree. His tapers, ferrules and grips were very similar to theirs and do not seem to maintain the same level of attention to detail or quality. This is chiefly a result that for a brief period of time as a result of his choice of glues Gillum rods experienced chronic de-lamination problems.

Nevertheless his rods still bring premium prices, partly because during his career as a rod builder less than 2000 rods were produced. They are scarce.

To identify his rods look for his lettered name on the early rods he build. Later rods used a stamp on the reel seat for identification.

Goodwin Granger Company
Founder Goodwin C. Granger began rod building just prior to 1920, the year he began commercial in Denver under the

name Goodwin Granger & Co. His rods became known for their high quality, due in part to their unique use of ammonia-tempered bamboo.

His first models were the Goodwin Rod, Granger Rod, Denver Special and the Colorado Special all were later renamed but remained a consistent part of the company's product line.

All the Goodwin Granger rods utilized nickel silver ferrules and reel seats, with only the quality of the cane, look of the windings and the number of guides used in each section differentiating between low and high end grades, which was how they referred to models.

The company's unique process of tempering the cane with a steam bath in ammonia gave the rods a unique color.

Hardy (UK)
This of course should be at the top of your "find" list when rummaging through the piles of otherwise pass-by-able stuff at yard sales. Hardy may arguably be the manufacturer of some of the finest fly rods ever made.

The company was founded in 1872 in Alnwick, Northumberland, England where William Hardy had already established himself as a gunsmith of some repute. Before long the business was given over exclusively to producing fishing tackle, the first love of William and his brother who had joined him in the company.

Heddon
James Heddon & Sons began in 1911 and was in continuous operation until 1956 producing some of the finest productions rods made during this period.

Rods produced before 1933 can be identified as "Heddon" was imprinted straight along the length of the rod. Prior to 1939 Heddon rods did not have the model name only the model number. After 1939 rods carried the model name, ferrule size and line weight designation.

Horrocks-Ibbotson
The Horrocks-Ibbotson company vied for the lead in the production of split cane manufactured rods for many years going toe to toe with both South Bend and Montague.

Horrocks was an immigrant from England who began his career as a clerk at a tackle company and was joined by an errand boy name Ibbotson. Together they later formed Horrocks-Ibbotson in 1894.

They manufactured rods in a wide variety of sizes, quality and price ranges for every sportsman. The highest quality rods like the Chancellor and the President had nickel silver ferrules. They made hundreds of models of rods from low to high end.

You will find decals fitted to rods that will aid in identification. One was a diamond with a UTK logo most often applied to the reel seat which they used from 1905 until World War I. A trout logo was subsequently used until about 1929 when it was then replaced by a double diamond with Utica, NY inside the diamond which was used until 1933.

An elaborate design followed which was a red H-I on a white diamond with two banners that read Fish Rod and Genuine Tonkin Cane.

In the 50's a rectangle with a small gold foil diamond was

used followed finally by a plain red diamond containing a white H-I.

Other hints for identification; H-I used white ink and the identification was written with the word running to the grip.

Montague

The Montague Rod Company was the largest producer of split cane rods for nearly 55 years. It began with a merger in 1900 with the Chubb Rod Company in Montague City, Massachusetts. They built a variety of rods beyond split cane fly rods with an emphasis on durability, which helps to explain why so many rods are still found in serviceable or restorable condition.

Orvis

In 1856 Charles Orvis and quickly was producing reels that were noted for both their quality and performance characteristics. The company developed a reputation excellence in outdoor products through a catalog, which was the forerunner of what we see today.

After the death of Charles his sons, Albert and Robert ran the company until it fell on hard times during the Depression when it was purchased by Dudley Corkran. Corkran hired master rod builder Wes Jordan who developed an impregnation process that vastly improved the weather and rot resistance nature of their fly rods.

In 1965 the company was purchased by Leigh Perkins and subsequently has become among the worlds leaders in the construction of high quality fly fishing equipment.

Paul Young Rod Company

A lifelong outdoor enthusiast, Paul Young in the early

1920's began his career as a rodmaker using a set of "V" blocks and a book on bamboo rod making.

His career lasted for more than forty years during which he became known for his patience and attention to detail.

Paul made rods for South Bend, Heddon Rod Co. and E.W. Edwards under the model names Prosperity and Depression rods.

Payne Rods
Payne rods are among the highest quality rods ever made famous for their near perfect tapers, which produced exceptional action combined with extraordinary beauty.

The E.F. Payne Rod Co. was founded in 1898 by Ed Payne. He had previously been a partner n the Thomas, Edwards and Payne Rod Co. which had been sold.

Four years after founding the company Ed's son, Jim, then 10 years old joined the company and started making rods. It turned out that young Jim was quite good at the craft and after his father's somewhat untimely death ten years later Jim assumed the helm of the company. He developed a process of flame tempering the bamboo producing a darkened blank which became the signature characteristic of Payne for years to come.

Pezon & Michel (F)
The company was begun when Pezon purchased a fishing tackle company in 1895.

When his son-in-law, Jean Michel took over the name changed to Pezon et Michel which upon acquiring the Garreau Company developed a line of split cane fly rods.

With the addition of the Pujol fly rod company their business begins to expand rapidly.
Eventually, the tide turns to financial difficulties and in 1975 Pezon & Michel is acquired by the Franchi Company. This acquisition is unable to turn the failing Pezon & Michel Co. around and so it is sold once more but until 1999 when Francois Hue took over the company and recommitted it to the production of quality split cane fly rods.

Phillipson

Bill Phillipson was a rod maker for the Goodwin Granger Co. until it closed just before World War II. He then started the Phillipson Rod and Tackle Co., producing his series of split cane rods in 1946. Phillipson was responsible for many improvements in the manufacture of rods including the nickel silver internal up locking reel seat.

Since Bill was almost without exception committed to performance rather than the beauty of his rods his critics showed little mercy. As a result of the particular glue the company used lines were sometimes evident in the finished rods that might have been eliminated had Phillipson chosen to use different and in Phillipson's view inferior performing glues. The distinctive dark purple that runs between strips of bamboo was a common feature of Phillipson rods.

Among the models Phillipson produced were the Paramount, Premium, Pacemaker, Paragon, Preferred and Peerless. In 1952 Phillipson introduced a travelling rod called the Smuggler, which was a four piece.
Under a private label Phillipson produced the Haywood Zephyr and the Ed M. Hunter Approved.

South Bend Rod Co.

Among the best know rod makers in the world, not just for

its split cane rods but for the full array of tackle for every variety of fishing.
Their bamboo rods were the epitome of what we think of as the manufactured rad. Their rods were extremely well made and many survived rugged use on pond and stream and are still being used.

Wesley Jordan, one of the most famous rod makers of his time and any other was a real innovator and left his mark on several companies. Best known for his work in the latter part of his career when he joined Orvis in Manchester, VT, Jordan was once an important part of the South Bend operation.

Jordan's rod making began as a favor to his friend

William Forsyth who when the two were on a fishing trip in Maine broke his rod. Forsyth, knowing that his friend was both an avid fly fisherman and accomplished at detail work talked Jordan into building him a replacement rod.

It took Jordan over a year during which time he learned everything he could about split cane rod construction and ultimately presented Forsyth with a rod that so impressed him that together they formed the Cross Rod Co. with third partner William Cross, a principal shareholder.

Jordan designed a milling machine that streamlined the process of rod building with bamboo. They specialized in rods of exceptional strength, focusing initially on tournament and saltwater trolling rods, leading to a company reputation for solid quality and affordable prices.

After the death of his partner Forsyth, Jordan moved to South Bend to oversee their rod production facility. He stayed for fifteen years and continued to refine the company's ability to manufacture good quality rods with low production costs.

His innovations allowed South Bend to successfully compete with other mass production rod makers of the time like Wright & McGill, Horrocks-Ibbotson, Union Hardware and Montague.

R.W. Summers
A contemporary rod builder living in Traverse City, Michigan Summers has been building rods since 1956

Thomas & Thomas
Thomas & Thomas was formed by the partnership of two brothers-in-law who began their rod making careers as a hobby. In 1972, the partners purchase equipment and a building in Greenfield, Massachusetts from rod maker Sewell Dunton, when in 1974 they took on partner Len Codella and moved the business to Turners Falls, Massachusetts.

The company was eventually sold to an Irish company, P. J. Carroll Co. Thomas & Thomas rods are still being produced and are among the most prized rods available.

So this gives us a good starting point. Brands which are not included might be considered of lesser quality; many were produced in large quantities and not with high standards.

And the value of an old bamboo rod is not only made by its intrinsic value but often by the rarity of the rods which have reached our days. So, both Garrison's, Harold "Pinky" Gillum, Lile Lynde Dickerson's rod all made very few rods

(Everett Garrison made about 650 pieces in his life, and about 25 at most per year) and so their value for collectors is higher, generally speaking.

Most vintage bamboo rods are not so valuable and reach a few hundreds dollars at auctions because there were made in the thousands for the mass market, and their quality was rather average or low.

For brother Bob, fisherman and companion extraordinaire!
Robert David Dougherty 1955 – 2002

Antiquarian and other sporting titles from
Hand Thrown Books

ALL ABOUT TROUT FISHING
J. A. Riddell - 1909

"As an angler who has spent most of twenty five seasons by the riverside my aim is to convey to the reader, in simple language, the outcome of actual experience, in the hope that beginners, and also more experienced anglers, may find some information that will enlighten and assist them in attaining better piscatorial results."

AMERICAN PARTRIDGE AND PHEASANT SHOOTING – 1877 – Frank Schley

Wherein the methods of hunting partridge, quail and ruffed grouse, tips on guns and dogs and the art of wing shooting are described. "Successful shooting is the ability to measure at a glance, 30 to 50 yards with certainty. Unless you learn to judge distances accurately when in the field, you will never become certain of stopping your birds."

CULTURE OF THE QUAIL
HOW TO RAISE QUAIL FOR PROFIT

Raising quail is a unique and interesting business, combining pleasure with few drawbacks. The quail is easily raised, cost very little to feed, are hardy, healthy and generally free from every contagious disease. The quail brings a better price than all other poultry providing for a decidedly profitable business having a good future before it.

DUCKING DAYS
1919 – An anthology

Narratives of duck hunting by famous outdoorsmen who had the good fortunate to have spent time on lakes, rivers and marshes during the Golden Age of hunting. "A Texas Duck Hunt" "Following the Redheads to the Gulf Coast" "On Missouri River Bars" "Duck Shooting on the Illinois River" more

DUCK SHOOTING AND HUNTING SKETCHES
1916 - William C. Hazelton

Narratives of Duck Hunting Experiences, Habits of Our Wild Fowl and Hunting Methods, Facts Concerning Migration, Breeding Grounds, Food and Articles about Some of Our Game Birds and Several Anecdotes on Hunting Dog Tales of the hunt from the Golden of Age of hunting on by-gone marshes, rivers and lakes.

FISHING AND SHOOTING SKETCHES
1909 – Grover Cleveland

This is a timeless collection of sporting tales by President Grover Cleveland who was both a dedicated hunter and fisherman; an experienced angler and excellent wing shooter. But he knew his shortcomings. On quail shooting, for instance he admitted. "I do not assume to be competent to give advice on shooting. I miss shots too often to undertake such a role."

FUR FEATHER & FIN – *Trout Series*
1904 – Alfred E. T. Watson

Anyone who is desirous of obtaining a fair share of piscatorial good fortune should take care that his fishing garb is sober of hue and not of a nature to attract the attention of the trout. Let your rod be light and gentle, and let not your line exceed three or four hairs at the most; but if you can attain to angle with one hair, you shall have more rises and catch more fish. *Trout Wisdom*

FUR FEATHER & FIN – *Snipe & Woodcock Series*
1903 – Alfred E. T. Watson

For the sportsman memories of upland hunts for either bird evokes arguments favoring one over the other. Such is the depth of feelings experienced when seeking sport with these little game birds. Fur Feather and Fin ***Snipe & Woodcock Series*** first published in 1903 explores the habits, haunts and shooting techniques of these elusive denizens of the uplands.

GAME FARMING
1915 – A Hercules Powder Company Publication

Game Farming provides step by step instructions on the breeding and preservation of quail, partridge, pheasant, wild duck and grouse. Contained in this extensive reference book is information to their natural feed, habitat, the control of natural enemies. It focuses on the need, based on the excesses of unchecked hunting practices for restoration of game through the application of responsible breeding practices.

JIST HUNTING
1921 – Ozark Ripley

"Ozark Ripley loves the outdoors, the far horizons and dogs. And every dog I have ever known loved Ozark. A man who loves dogs and is loved by dogs always rings true." Ozark shares his experiences with rod, gun and old mother earth immersed in the outdoors with only frying pan, a bag of flour, a bit of bacon, a blanket, rushing, streams, wind kissed waters, and woodland trails.

LAKE FIELD AND FORREST
1899 – Frank A. Bates

A wonderful collection of stories by self proclaimed "sportsman-naturalist" Frank Bates. Published in 1899 his stories paint a lavish picture of a golden era of hunting and fishing that thankfully has been preserved through the journals and writings of sportsmen like Bates of that time.

PHEASANT FARMING
A DETAILED "HOW TO"

IN AMERICA we have been very wasteful of our natural our resources. This is especially the case in the destruction of our game birds.
That we must produce, if we would destroy has finally dawned on us. Propagation is the only solution of the future game supply problem.

PRACTICAL DRY FLY FISHING
1912 - Emlyn M. Gill

The subject has been fully covered by a number of expert writers who have lived in the home of the dry-fly, England.

With the exception of a few magazine articles, there has been little American Literature upon the subject. This work is confined to the floating fly. The beauties of nature, one of the chief attractions of a day on the trout stream, are left to the poetic pens of English literature.

SCATTERGUN SKETCHES
1922 – Horatio Bigelow

WHEN business binds and you can't seem to get away on that long anticipated shooting trip, you can find relief in the "Call of the Wild". When gathered around the camp-fire how often have you heard the "old timers" spin the yarns that linger with you? These are those yarns from long ago told with wit and an eye for detail which will carry you back.

SPECKLED BROOK TROUT
1902 – Various authors

The brook trout has long held a special place in the hearts and minds of anglers. Lavishly illustrated this volume, a collection from the pens of a number of well known writers, begins by supplying general information on the wily brookie, before moving on to discuss habitat, habits and angling methods then finally culinary considerations.

TALES OF DUCK AND GOOSE SHOOTING
1922 – William C. Hazelton

Whether hunted for food or to show skill with a gun some imperative causes man reject all creature comforts, brave exposure to nasty weather, or risk the danger of accidental mutilation or death. Along with the duck season comes a longing to fondle a gun and sit staring at the ammunition box. This wonderful collection recounts stories from the golden era of water fowling.

THE ART OF WING SHOOTING
1895 – William Bruce Leffingwell

The Art of Wing Shooting is a practical treatise on the use of the shot gun. Illustrated by sketches and easy to read it guides you to become an expert shot. It contains a complete expose of the scientific use of the shot gun along with an examination of the habits and resorts of game birds and waterfowl. And how to become a proficient inanimate target shot.

THE BOYS BOOK OF HUNTING AND FISHING
1914 – Warren H. Miller

"There is but one excuse for the men of to-day and that is to prepare boys by instilling in them an enduring appreciation for the great outdoors; undoubtedly a good thing." This work is devoted to the proper use of rod and gun to provide an opportunity to go to the open for their games and recreation with the helping hand of an exhaustive book on sports of the outdoor world.

THE IDYL OF THE SPLIT BAMBOO
1920 – George Parker Holden

The fisherman's transcendent implement is his rod. While few anglers might undertake making a split cane rod it requires little to convince anyone that fishermen love to tinker with their tackle. If you can make a rod you certainly can fix one. Building a split-bamboo rod is an operation in overcoming those particular difficulties in handling and working bamboo which give the most trouble

THE SPORTING DOG
1904 – Joseph A. Graham

It's commonly conceded that Great Britain provided the stock all our dogs of sporting breed. So how do they differ from the British dogs? Reduced to the simplest terms they are faster, lighter and quicker in action." *The Sporting Dog*" is a fascinating study of the development of the American hunting dog.

TRAINING THE HUNTING DOG
1901 – B. Waters

Dog training, considered as an art, has no mysteries, no insurmountable obstacles, and unfortunately no short cuts. It is a result of patient schooling analogous to that employed in the training a child. In this case however the trainees are being prepared for limited service in the pursuit of game. Full of practical, usable, effective training methods it is as relevant today as it was 100 years ago.

TROUT FISHING FOR BEGINNERS
Richard Clapham

The perfect gift for either the beginning trout angler or the seasoned angler who can occasionally use a gentle reminder of how often ignoring the basics of the sport can lead to an empty creel. This is a wonderful little classic that should be a part of every sportsman's library.

TROUT FISHING IN AMERICA
1914 – Charles Zibeon Southard

The author attempts to settle once and for all the raging controversy over whether it is better to embrace the dry fly or wet fly school of fly fishing. And while this topic remains unresolved this classic is a richly warm and extensively useful volume on virtually every aspect of fly fishing for trout. From rod to reel, from line to leader no stone in the stream is left unturned.

THE WILDERNESS HOME
1908 – Oliver Kemp

IF you love the out-of-doors, this book was written for you, to crystallize and bring into reality that vague longing which you have felt for a lodge in the wilderness.

Somewhere the trail has led you to the ideal spot in the deep forest, by the shores of a smiling lake or within sound of the murmuring waters.

WING SHOOTING
1881 – Anonymous

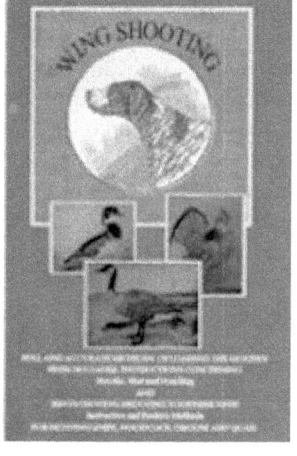

The author in "Wing Shooting" provides full directions for the various methods of loading the modern breach-loader, along with instructions concerning powder, shot and wadding. Also covered are general hints on wing shooting together with instructive and positive methods for hunting snipe, woodcock, grouse and quail.

WOODCOCK SHOOTING
1908 – Edmund Davis

Lazy days spent in the uplands inevitably bring a closer connection with nature; especially when your sport is seeking that wily little game bird, the woodcock. For the woodcock reassures us that the brooks are still dancing merrily through the woods and are on their way to sweet scented meadows. So it is, the woodcock brings joy to the lovers of forest, cover and stream.

Additional sporting titles available on Amazon
IF HE'S DEAD NOW HE'LL BE DEAD IN THE MORNING
2012 – J. C. Dougherty

Tales of full creels, full waders and the all too occasional perfect point from a snazzy setter. Revisit with the author crisp autumn days wandering bird-less through the woods, or sunny spring afternoons casting about for un-cooperative trout. These are stories of life-long friends and life-long laughs. Journal of a Somewhat Amusing Outdoor Life is the perfect gift for the sportsman in your life.

AN EDIBLE MEMOIR   2014 -   J. C. Dougherty

Where north meets south; from grits to game birds Recipes and tall tales about the big ones that got away and the collard greens that couldn't. Black Eye Pea Fritters with Onion Jam ~ Woodcock Pie ~ Cajun Fried Bullfrog ~ Hush Puppies ~ Fried Grits ~ Duck Soup with White Beans ~ Fried Catfish Southern Fried Chicken ~ Okra Fried to within an inch of its life!

THE ART OF RESTORING SPLIT CANE FLY RODS.
2012 – J. C. Dougherty

Split cane bamboo fly rods are not for everyone, some people are too addicted to high tech. Bamboo rods only warm the heart and are in tune with the rhythms of the rivers streams and lakes they touch. And there's little else that is as satisfying as bringing one of these classic rods back to life. Advice, tips and instructions on how to repair cracks, splits broken ferrules cork grip and more.

Hand Thrown Books
West Newbury, MA
www.handthrownbooks.com

www.ingramcontent.com/pod-product-compliance
Lightning Source LLC
Chambersburg PA
CBHW070326100426
42743CB00011B/2575